TYPING IN THE DARK

Saundra Sharp

With the photography of
Nathaniel Bellamy, Gerald Cyrus,
Calvin Hicks, and Adele Hodge

GW00506694

HARLEM RIVER PRESS
New York City

Published for HARLEM RIVER PRESS by:
WRITERS & READERS PUBLISHING, INC.
P.O. Box 461, Village Station,
New York, New York 10014

Acknowledgments:
page 3 quotation, from "The Serapis Meditation" by Dr. Alfred M. Ligon,
Aquarian Spiritual Center

Lyrics from "Hey, Mann" by Bernice Johnson Reagon, "Sweet Honey In
The Rock," Songtalk Publishing Co., BMI, © 1976

Lyrics from "On Broadway" by Mann, Weil, Leiber & Stoller, Screen
Gems-EMI Music, © 1962

Lyrics from "Compared to What" by Gene McDaniels, Lonport Publish-
ing Co., BMI, © 1968

Lyrics from "Soweto Blues" by Hugh Masekela and Stanley Kwesi Todd.
We've Got Rhythm Music, Inc. & Irving Music, Inc. © 1977

Some poems previously published in the anthology *Say That The River
Turns* (Third World Press) and Black Elegance magazine.

CIP: 91-071281

ISBN 0-86316-305-X (Paperback)
ISBN 0-86316-300-9 (Hardcover)

Manufactured in the United States of America

9 8 7 6 5 4 3 2 1   96 95 94 93 92 91

CONTENTS

dedicated to my personal, living angels

(Aunt) Juanita Rollins

Sarah and George Livingston

Mrs. Agnes Davis

*who have made sure the poet
could afford the necessities:
time to work, gas in Sassafras,
writing munchies, the rent,
typewriter ribbons and ice cream*

*and for Arnold, 1955-1990,
who wore words like diamonds
and ate poems for breakfast*

1
Typing In The Dark

"I am Black as the night from which
the light of a new day descends . . . "

There is still the

    possibility

       of music

when I can make you smile

Hello my Friend

    Rest yourself

       Stay awhile

WE STILL WRITE LOVE POEMS

We still write love poems
because in the deepest
most resonant part
of our collective spirit
We won't let love
be taken away from us.

because it keeps hate
from getting out of hand
because We have
tenure in forgiveness
and tenderness
as plentiful as mornings.

so pin a poem to the lynching tree
dance a dance for the spirits at sea

give honor to the tribes of Surinam
sound the horn for the Bloods of 'Nam

beat the drum for Amistad
blow the sax for Soledad

ring the bell for the Black Star Line
create a praisesong for the Little Rock 9

write rhyme for the daughters of Birmingham
make words dance on the graves of Klan

haiku for the minds that went away
sing the song for Marvin Gaye

stomp down strong for Soweto
throw the bones for old Jim Crow

lay hands on Boston and Bensonhurst
chant a chant for democracy's curse

juba back the pain, the fear
record the way of our survival here

We still write love poems
because it heals us
coming slow in the day
or late in the life
bandaging pain and absence

because love is the ground on which
our soul dances
the breath of the womb
the silence hovering over the grave
We still write love poems.

GERALD CYRUS

L.A./D.C. CONNECTION

1.

If I could touch you now
from this far place
I'd wrap you in raiments of
        windlight
moon dust swirling at your hips
sun jewels sparkling
in the air
we share
together

If I could touch you now
from this far space
I'd perfume your nest
with the sweet memory
of our togetherness

If I could touch you now
from across the room
I'd brush you
with my softness
dance on your voice
with tongue tied tonals
of rain shine
    sweet time

If I could touch you now
        and I can,
        and I *can,*
        and I can.

2.

I need your voice
in my day
it connects me
its familiar notes
are heart insurance
for my spirit
which celebrates you
for my eyes
that touch you
for my pulse
that breathes with you

I need your voice
in my day

I need your voice
in my night

telling me
it's time to rest
I want your voice
in my nest.

3.

You take the
frazzle edged ends of
my me
and weave them
into security

4.

you are
a watercolor
splashed
        between
my phone calls
        &
lists of things to do

5.

sometimes
when I walk
into the closet
to snatch my
gray   sweater
I want to stay there

sit on the floor
huddled
quiet
in the dark
maybe
when I come out
things   will
          have
changed

6.

I lost you somewhere

you're not in the kitchen
telling me what not to eat
you're not by the box
sharing Randy Crawford's love songs

was it talking money?
are we both very tired?

you're not in the
passenger seat of my car
you're not in the purple chair
waiting for me to get through

is it the moon?
the nature of society?
or just that I watched
          the six o'clock news . . . .

I lost you somewhere
these last few days . . . .

I'll take a shower

perhaps you're
waiting for me there.

7.

If you disconnect Us
then I am
naked out there
          out there open and closed
stripped of the protective
warm
that moved me
through the world with you

if you disconnect Us
then I am
all
               inside   again
hiding
to keep from being out there
naked
inside, quiet
inside talking to myself
because

i don't know
who new
who old
to talk to
who to trust
and what is there to say?

my line
               goes dead.

again.

if you disconnect Us
then i am
out there
hugging myself
floating
        between
   fear
   and
   flawed imagination.

NATHANIEL BELLAMY

SEVERED WHISPERS

silence like shocking news
silence like severed whispers
silence like a broken prayer

head   echoes

      the sound of your smile

        echoes   the

      drumbeat of your laugh

silence like dried blood
silence like cotton words
silence like the known in
      "cause of death unknown"

WORLD CHAMPION CUCUMBER

Sistuh grew it
she did
biggest cucumber
in the country

"I just did it,"
she did
"Grew it with some Miracle Gro."

I tried it
I did
sprinkled Miracle Gro
over my layered life

and waited
I did
to see if my
biggest ever life
would end up on TV
or in a salad.

TYPING IN THE DARK

you said the film was great
then I said I saw it --- I was in school
when I saw it
and you said
then I said
and what was it I really wanted
to say to you?
> You make me feel like a soft smile
> Come here.
> Wash your face in my touch.

the phone was almost ringing
and you said it wasn't working right
then I said they never do
and you said we should live without them
then I said
and what was it I really wanted
to say to you?
> that I need
> > need to be heard by you
> if you could hear my scream
> > it would lie down and roll away.

then you said what all our problem was
and I said we'd get it together eventually
then you said that apathy was killing us
and I said
and it wasn't that kind of life and death
> I wanted to talk about
> I am dying
> > > of loneliness
> and I wanted to ask you
> > (under the pretense of sharing a poem)
> can you save me?

then you said
then I said
and I left
sat on top of a parking lot
     wondering what sweet foolish
     feeling
made me think I could talk to you?

'Cause you can talk circles around life, too
yeah,   can talk circles around life, too
Am I running out of ribbon?
     running out of reason?   typing in the dark
Is someone watching my eyes unspark?
Is someone listening to my echo?

WONDERS

or, Crisis Thoughts Collected
In The Unemployment Office

Wonder how much it *costs* to pass a law against
   stealing babies?

Wonder how the country's founders figured
   that Africans could grow from no person
   to 3/5ths of a person?

Wonder how you tell the difference between a
   holocaust and American-style slavery?

Wonder why pictorial sex always has the woman
   undressed and the man dressed?

Wonder if Thomas Jefferson's wife knew he was
   Black?

Wonder how Columbus felt when he "discovered"
   some colored folks were already here?

Wonder why bodies don't come with instructions?

Wonder how, being inherently inferior and all that,
   Black folks produced a DuBois and a Drew, a
   Robeson and a Rillieux, an Ida B. and a Baldwin
   . . . . in just the first 100 years out of slavery?

Wonder if Jefferson's Black mistress (who loved
   white men) knew he was Black?

Wonder why women can't stop war?

Wonder how blood that's only 1/10th Black gets
   to be so powerfully brown in the light? /
   or light in the brown?

Wonder why I'm wiser now that three of my wisdom
   teeth are gone?

19

PRAYER FOR HAROLD WASHINGTON

I fear for you,
Harold Washington.
In the fleeting moments
between the phone and
        taking laundry from the dryer
I feel a sharp pain of fear for you.
And though I am not given to praying,
I pray for you.

I fear for you,
Harold Washington.
Miss my exit from the freeway
because I hear my grandmother singing
Were You There? when they crucified
And though I am not given to praying,
I pray for you.

        Like red-lined property,
        the value of your life
        depreciated sharply
        when you dared move
        into a new neighborhood.
        You are among the numbered now
        You are among the chosen and the damned
        And I feel powerless to protect you
                feel powerless to protect you.

It is an angry prayer
I must now fear for you
the same as my mother,
and her mother
and hers drew
a breath of fear
with every breath of love.

But fear,
       they say,
is a weakening process

     so I clench my fist
     polish my gun
     carry Malcolm in my purse
     yet
     check my black veiled hat
            in the closet
     and finding nothing else to do
     I pray for you.

But my sweet jesus, my allah,
    pretty buddah,
           my rah
   jah!   jah!
    jah!

It is my fear that talks for me,
and I mask it in my prayer,
My every moment prayer for you,
Harold Washington.

              4/83

Harold Washington (1922-1987) was the first
African-American mayor of the city of Chicago.

SPACE AVAILABLE

space

    left by

intensely bright
        expansive space
                left by

    Kathleen Collins

incredible view with vision

space

for lease

        space to
             move
   around in
two stories
two stories

       space left
       left space

       left by James Baldwin

how will we decorate

       with plants
       with paints
       with words

all this empty space?

DOUBLE EXPOSURE

in the mirror
she holds on
again

      if u can't leave
      u can't stay here
      get off my face!

if i leave this room
people will
see i am
not my own face

      if u can't leave
      u can't stay here
      get off my face!

she stays,
much too comfortable

      i left
      to flee your
      hand-me-down fears
      our answers
      no longer matched

she stays, as if i am
still on duty
in Her image

      i am not you anymore
      i am my own collection of
      gifts and errors

      so woman spirit
      if u can't leave
      u can't stay here

and finally, she moves off
(as in retiring to Her room
                        after a trying day)

                    don't you
                    remember
                    the sunshiny days?

i smooth in the camouflage
        smudge the brown red rouge
            assemble it all
                hoping
                    if u can't leave
hoping to hold on
                    if u can't leave
to my own face
                    u can't stay here
for a few days
                    get off my face!
please?

BACK INSIDE HERSELF

She's going back inside herself
        back inside herself
She's going back inside herself
        back inside herself

away from large talk on small issues
from plastic face and form
from catered smiles winced with pain

away from gossip
and lazy lovers
from decoration that is
        at cross purpose with her beauty

She's going back inside herself
        back inside herself
She's going back inside herself
        back inside herself

away from organized hate
and legislated freedom
from self inflicted disease
from death by bureaucracy

away from spirit killers
from diminished grace
from pleasures unpromised

away from hollyweird
from people who don't hear her
        don't hear her
        don't hear her need
      and don't need her here!

She's going back inside herself
        back inside herself
She's going back inside herself
        back inside herself

inside herself
talking to herself
in herself
she will
sing Sweet Honey
speak in Biko
dance to thunder
practice Malcolm
hear unwritten songs
create new answers
know universal law
and rearrange the order of things
inside herself
talking to herself
in herself

They see her going
(those who can)
and expect she'll come back
like a wham-a-ma-zam!
a hot mama jahma
fantasy of a real wonda woman
'cause they don't understand
she *was* a wonda woman
when she went
back inside herself

She's going back inside herself
back inside herself
She's going back inside herself
back inside herself

back inside herself
in herself
she be
silk soft
easing through the seams of leaves

she be
silver wet
dispensing dew

she be
the sulpher tipped match
lighting sun

she be
spun cocoa
slipping across the
tip of your tongue

sistuh gods
flowing through her
inside her
she be
pure power
pure power
pure power
that consumes you
in the need to be
            where she is:

back inside
        inside herself
                herself.

5/83

2
Signifyin'

SAUNDRA SHARP

I AM NOT AN AFRICAN QUEEN

I am *not* an "African Queen."

I've got pimples
pee
promises
dirty laundry
my car has cancer
my rent is due 12 x a year.

I am *not* an African Queen.
I grow yams at the corner bodega
the hair swinging in my cornrows
comes from Hong Kong
my warriors rally
on the freeway at rush hour
and I am not in command . . . .

My body is wrapped in 50% polyester
my dandruff needs scratching
my French is lacking
and I sometimes
(forgive me)
forget what you
are calling yourself now.

I am not an African Queen
just a simple
wombman
trying to maneuver a planet.

my mind craves food not in season
can you feed me?

I'm a background doo-wop
can you carry the lead?

do you do windows
or only praisesongs?
do you do hugs?
can you hold my blood in the night?

Don't ask me to be royal beyond my means
'cause I deal in the realness of my dreams
I am not an African Queen
give *me* the pedestal
electric bill came yesterday
I can use the firewood.

IT'S THE LAW
a rap poem

You can learn about the state of the U.S.A.
By the laws we have on the books today.
The rules we break are the laws we make
The things that we fear, we legislate.

We got laws designed to keep folks in line
Laws for what happens when you lose your mind
Laws against stealing, laws against feeling,
The laws we have are a definite sign
That our vision of love is going blind.
(They probably got a law against this rhyme.)
Unh-hunh . . . . .

We got laws for cool cats & laws for dirty dogs
Laws about where you can park your hog
Laws against your mama and your papa, too
Even got a law to make the laws come true.

It's against the law to hurt an ol' lady,
It's against the law to steal a little baby,
The laws we make are what we do to each other
There is no law to make brother love brother
Hmmm . . . .

Now this respect thang is hard for some folks to do
They don't respect themselves
          so they can't respect you
This is the word we should get around ---
These are the rules: we gonna run 'em on down.
Listen up!:

It ain't enough to be cute,
It ain't enough to be tough
You gotta walk tall
You gotta strut your stuff

You gotta learn to read, you gotta learn to write
Get the tools you need to win this fight
Get your common sense down off the shelf
Start in the mirror . . . . Respect your Self!

When you respect yourself you keep your body clean
You walk tall, walk gentle, don't have to be mean
You keep your mind well fed, you keep a clear head
And you think 'bout who you let in your bed ---
Unh-hunh . . . . . .

When you respect yourself you come to understand
That your body is a temple for a natural plan
It's against that plan to use drugs or dope ---
Use your heart and your mind when you need to cope . . .
It's the law!

We got laws that got started in '86
And laws made back when the Indians got kicked
If we want these laws to go out of favor
Then we've got to change our behavior

Change what!? you say, well let's take a look
How did the laws get on the books? Yeah.
I said it up front but let's get tougher
The laws we make are what we do to each other

If you never shoot at me then I don't need
A law to keep you from shooting at me, do you see?
There's a universal law that's tried and true
Says Don't do to me ---
What you don't want done to you
Unh-hunh!
Don't do to me ---
What you don't want done to you
It's the law!

HOMED

Giving money is easy
She is not easy

She parks her car
pleased that it is modest
the people will know
she is of them,
not above them

Her entrance creates graciousness
where none is necessary
her limited smile
announces that she understands

She brings bread,
explains how the clothes have been
mended with lye

She promises more

Leaving, she
s t r e t ches toward her haven
swelled with goodness
and brightfully relieved!
that no one
has asked her
to bring
one of the homeless
home

SAUNDRA SHARP

I must . . . .

I must get back to writing political poems.
I must get back to writing political poems.

Reagan is playing his most power full role

I must get back to writing political poems.
I must get back to writing political po---

Haitians are swimming to my shores,
the life rafts are filled with jelly beans.

I must get back to writing politi---

South Africa gave its natives a Black TV station:
    the first segregated talking box

I must get back to write ---

Sister Sledge has gone from
                "We Are Family"
    to "All American Girls"
    and Donna Summer is on the block

I must get bac---

Black people think they're going to the moon . . . *too!*

I must . . .

I must . . . . . .

    (whoops)

        too

          late.

            '82

37

LADY PERFECT

She spent her whole life
becoming perfect
becoming perfect for love
for love
that would be coming.

At some point
She came to learn
perfection
is not required for love
for love
that would be coming.

But in the absence
of love's coming
she continued to pursue
perfection
perfection for love
that would be coming
After all,
there must be something
to show
for such a lengthy quest
for love
for love
that would be coming. . . .

I'm

gonna

marry

myself

stay

home

and

be

a

housewife.

CALVIN R. HICKS

We always kiss when I'm leaving

And I can't help but wonder

If he's glad to see me go

I know he doesn't realize

We always kiss goodbye ---

We never kiss hello.

IN THE BEGINNING THERE WAS NO TELEVISION

In the beginning
there was no television.
I say, in the beginning
there was no television.

Black folks sang and planned,
children chased lightnin' bugs,
lovers held hands on the porch,
elders told stories that were real.
There was cooking and new babies and
daily they gathered to share company.
Those with intuition
watched the world through third I vision.

And in a quick breath of time
there came onto the planet earth
a Box, that talked.
And they called it Radio.

And the Box that talked begat
a Box that walked and talked.
And they called it Tele Vision.

Man rushed to prance and dance on the
Box that walked and talked.
Darktown's dapper were first in line,
the Apollo was right on time
with "Uptown Jubilee!" It was 1949.

Thus was born into the language the
stunning scream: "OU, LOOK! THERE'S
SOME COLORED PEOPLE ON TEE VEE!"

And from that day to this there has been
        confusion.

For the Box begat the maids Beulah and Oriole
        some said they were too loud
        some said they were good maids

some said they were too black
some said "But they're getting paid."
And we all watched.

And Beulah begat Amos, Kingfish and Andy
some said they were stupid
some said they were funny
some said "They're not like the Negroes
I know."
some said "But they're making money!"
And we all watched.

And Kingfish begat the domestic Rochester,
some said
"He dignifies the work we do."
some said
"He's just Jack Benny's maid, his fool."
And we all watched.

On still summer evenings
the songbirds would show:
Hazel Scott, Billy Daniels,
especially Nat King Cole.
some said
"Look how the world imitates our stance!"
some said
"All niggers can do is sing and dance."
And we all watched.

Then,
for three years,
there were no Black folks on television.
I say, for three years
no Black folks were on Tee Vee,
at least, none you could see regularly.
And we all watched.
Anyway.

The silence was broken
When Leslie sang along with Mitch

some said "Sweet music,"
some said "White Folks' music."
And we all watched.

On the east side and on the west side
Cicely waved her social wand
    some said
    "At last! An educated Black woman
    is on the air."
    but some said
    "Why don't that girl do somethin'
    'bout that nappy hair!"
And we all watched.

Now Black folks sang and planned,
children made picket signs,
lovers went off to ride freedom buses,
elders told stories of voting the first time.
There was cooking and new babies and
nightly they huddled to watch
the dogs attack and the whips crack,
the marchers' concern as the crosses burned.
They saw themselves as the evening news.
Those with ancestral missions
watched the Box with fearless vision.

It was the worst of times
It was the blackest of times
It begat the Good Times.

For the Box conceded that
the Colorful People were (perhaps)
qualified to enter the treacherous race
for the American Dream
(if they took their time).

And in their time
if you had just One Life to Live
and knew the way to Sesame St.
you could get a seat in Room 222
watching Julia race to reach the Dream.

In their time
you could run the race
Barefoot in the Park policed by
Shaft, Christie Love and Cosby the spy.
The Mod Squad guarded the ribbon
and even the Rookies knew
when to move the marker
        to change the rules
        to insure that the NYPD
        would always win.

In their time
those with peculiarly Different strokes
saw the race as a mission Impossible,
tore the numbers off their chests
and laid bets on the conditions of surrender.
Those who could not endure the ordeal
took the Soul Train back to Palmerstown
where the little Rascals and a misspelled Lt. Uhura
offered shade under the White Shadow
And we all watched.
We watched and we watched until we grew Roots.
        some said
        "Now America will understand
        the depth of our struggle in this land."
        some said
        "The master's too sweet, the slave's too
                brave
        It wasn't like that back in slavery days."

The Box begat a new plantation called Beulah Land
where the Jeffersons and Sanford's son
were All in the same Family,
where the field slaves were extinct
and only a few mismodeled T. hands were needed,
needed to pull the trigger
        to push the needle
        to change the channel

And because we thought it was What's Happenin'
the children went dancing in the streets

each a solo unto themselves
babies made love made babies, while
upward mobility parents made
appointments to meet themselves.
The elders, left alone,
whispered the prophecies
to no one.
Those with history's wisdom
watched a people abandon their vision

But once a week,
    (On Thursday, usually, around eight)
we gathered in scattered company

And
we
all
watched.

12/86
Non-Violent Family Film Festival
The King Center, Atlanta

YET YOU WORSHIP ME

You fear my power
            yet you worship me
you castrate my men
            yet you worship me
you suffer my wisdom
you refuse to honor Krishna while
you remake me with missionaries
            yet you worship me

you make suntans a status symbol
            you imitate me
you fantasize tall, dark & handsome
            you make love with me
you dip your hip in my dance
you are baptized in my music
you study my rhythm and when convenient
            you pass for me

you pay to avoid my neighborhood
            yet you worship me
you are threatened by my offspring
            yet you worship me
you negate my history
you pollute my life force and
you plant genocide on my doorstep
            yet you worship me

You are all in my blackness
and my blackness is all in you
the Pope kisses my feet
            I am the Black Madonna
I dance in my own temple
            I am the Black Tie Ball
I am larger than life
            I am the Black Sea
I am incomprehensible
            I am the Black Forest
I ride the fierce wind of rebellion
            I am the Black Stallion

Bake 'Til Golden Brown.
Fly Delta To Mexico.

SAUNDRA SHARP

You are all in my blackness
and my blackness is all in you
I am the wine you prize
            I am "the darker the berry"
I gamble with your sincerity
            I am the Black Jack dealer
I am 9/10ths of your seed
            I am the Black child
I am the first world out of place
            I am your third eye
I am your classiest color
            I am basic Black

And you worship me.

So what *is* the problem??

ADELE HODGE

RELATIVE TO WHAT?

(Cholesterol is announced as "the number one threat to public health.")

smog
sexual rape
sniper killings
meat hormones
designer tap water
crossfire of gang wars
germicide experiments
Klan membership on credit
CIA cop running the country
experimental brain manipulation
denied health care by the government
political mandates from the unconscious

death

by

cholesterol?

I

should

be

so

lucky

JESSE JESUS

written after my first encounter with the process
of selecting presidential convention delegates '88

Be Jesus, Jesse
Be Jesus, Jesse

Jesse save the farm
Jesse save the young
Jesse save the addict
Jesse heal the gangs
Jesse protect the children
Jesse stop the racists
Jesse multiply the fish
Jesse turn water into wine
           war into wisdom.

Be Jesus, Jesse
Be Jesus, Jesse
We who are hungry
for maps
and methods
to take us
where? . . . .
          where? . . .

out of debt
    Jesse be a job
out of pain
    Jesse be a cure
out of hunger
    Jesse be a welfare check
out of hate
    Jesse be a healer
out of despair
    Jesse be a rainbow

When we are out of hope
Please be Jesus, Jesse
be all the things
we are unwilling to be
ourselves.

heal us
help us
lead us
save us
and above all
if you fail us
be crucified, Jesse
(for leaving a "vacant" sign
in the room we meant for Jesus)

Yeah,
Be all we need
Be Jesus, Jesse,
But be careful.

HOLLYWOOD AUDITIONS

Enough of this!
I'll just go write a poem.
a poem that will just *be*
be gloriously
            gorgeously me

and no one
can tell my poem that it's
too short
or too tall
or too dark
or too young
or too old
or too Black
or too not Black enough

my poem will curl dread
        but it won't wig
it will be hairy
        but it won't jerri
it will sound Black
        but it won't rap

my poem will not be cast
        it will not be cut
        it will not do windows
        or Pearl Bailey imitations
        it won't need to be directed
        and it will not be changed to White.

it cannot be contained
and it will not be polite

my poem will just *be*
        be gloriously
            georgeously
                me!

I AM THE BODY
   (notes from the original war)

I am the body.
I choose between 81 brands of shampoo,
187 colors of nail polish
and a diet for each week I spend on the planet
I am the body beautiful.

I am the body.
I can be real sweet, semi-sweet,
          nutra-sweet, saccharin sweet
I rage against cholesterol
while supporting a billion
hamburger stands worldwide
I am the body nourished.
Given a choice of 32 brands of laxatives
I am the body cleansed.

I am the body.
I have 20/20 vision
I choose from 75 television channels and
          watch them all
Yet I cannot see
I am the body enlightened.

I am the temple.
I choose between 36 major religions
and spend 25 billion a year embracing them
I am the body blessed

I choose to create,
I create ways to destroy
I am the body at war.

I am the lover.
I choose passion over pride,
fire over ashes,
security in lieu of living.
In love, I choose
          to imitate myself
therefore

I am the body impregnated
I can do it with you
                    by myself
                    inside me
                    outside myself
                    by love or number
                    by intimacy or sperm bank
                    in test tubes and gardens
                    in wombs of other women

          and you say I have no choice?

     yet you say I have no choice?

you say I have no choice??

*The television special "Paul Simon's Graceland: The
African Concert" premiered on cable May 16, 1987.
I watched it at a private*

GRACELAND VIDEO PARTY

> *"Soweto blues,*
> *Soweto blues,*
> *Soweto blues,*
> *Soweto blues. . . ."*

So my ex-husband said he wasn't going to . . .
until . . .
and then, Well
I couldn't believe it!   Girl!

> *"Children were flying, bullets dying*
> *The mothers screaming and a crying . . .*
> *The fathers were working in the city . . ."*

Well if he does it again, man,
I'm gonna have to go to Dick and
deal with it.
Yeah.
I mean, it was clearly *my* sale
I spent an hour with the man.

> *"Nkosi sikelela i-Africa . . ."*

Throw me one of them beers.
Damn! who drank up all the wine?!

> *"Maluphoakanyisw' uphondo lwayo . . ."*

You paid how much?! $1.49 a piece?
It's cheaper by the bucket.
Golden Bird, dude.   By the bucket for twelve

> *"Woza Moyo . . ."*

There's a little place over on Slauson
where you can get a bucket of fried chicken
for about ten dollars.
Really!?

"*Woza Moyo. . . .*"

So who's coming over tomorrow?
What's tomorrow?
The Celtics, baby.   10 a.m.

"*Woza Moyo oyingowele. . . .*"

Right on. Might as well stay all night.

"*Nkosi Sikelela. . . .*"

(   )

They all laughed when I left.
Tears rolled down my back.

"*Soweto blues,*
Soweto blues,
Soweto blues,
Soweto blues. . . ."

3
Singing

CALVIN R. HICKS

CULTURAL LOVE

i got a jones
for your bones

say
i got a jones
for your bones

got a 'preciation attitude
'bout you
comes down on me
when i see how u do

all day long
i wanna drop a dime
'cause u on the video screen
of my mind

i got a jones
for your bones

get high
off your sigh

got a nose
for your toes

mm-hmmmm
mm-hmmmm
mm-hmmmm

say
i got a jones
for your bones

COME SUNDAY

I keep removing him
from my bed
from my bath
from my deep reservoir
of possibilities
still, he is all
      "Hey, Man . . . . . .
over the place
      . . . what you doin' in here?"

yesterday
forced him out of the kitchen
today
rescinded his possibilities
by Sadiday
will have reclaimed control

then
Sun day here he comes
Sun day
sucking my ear
and being wonderful
all over the place

Have you met Miss Brooks?

i came breathless to meet her,
imagining
this grand grandmother
           sensible shoes
duster of family pictures
           strand of pearls
recorder of negroness
           organized papers
mother of Annie Allen
           touch of gray
knighted lady of prizes
           delicate strength

i came faint to meet her,
imagining
this farmer of
bean eaters and wordworkers

Mecca was waiting
she real cool
blue jeans
combat boots
red socks
kinked hair
levis lady
leading the word revolution

in celebration of
Sistuh Gwendolyn's
70th birthday, 1987

63

1-800-BLK-HIST

*(for the opening of the National Afro-American Museum
and Cultural Center, Wilberforce, Ohio, April 15, 1988)*

1-800-BLK-HIST
This is gonna be some par-tee
the word goes out by drum, by phone,
by Black Dispatch: "Ya'll come on home!"
A family that had disappeared
Would be resurrected this 88th year.

A site is chosen, a spirit home
Right on the Underground Railroad
The family is summoned to this special place
To bring their singular light and grace.

A washboard is the first to show
Singing "Lord, wash me whiter than snow."
The Maytag wringer is right on time
Soon curtains flutter from the line.

Excitement is high, the time is nigh,
A cast iron skillet starts to fry
A thousand chickens, while nearby
Candied yams turn up their nose
At the stink caused by some pigs' feet toes.

Some come early to decorate . . .
A doily done with tatted lace,
A barber pole, a Duncanson landscape,
A Jim Crow sign that knows its place.

Medals of war and photographs,
Masonic emblems and Dresden glass,
Annie Allen arrives at three
With a Pulitzer for the mantlepiece.

From 30 cities country wide
They come back home with joyous pride
3000 strong, plus a hundred or two,
They crowd into the soft lit rooms.

Some 78's step in like gold
Carrying Dinah, the Duke and Nat King Cole
A buffalo nickel goes in a slot
That gets a start from the bright juke box
Where Maybelline and Hound Dog do the stroll---
Lordy, Lordy, let the good times roll!

A hat comes in that once was used
By Meredith from Ol' Miss U.
A curling iron is pressed between
A cotton sack and a treadle machine.

They're even having a rousing time
Back in the library on shelf nine
Where books by Robeson and DuBois
Are united again in prophetic joy.

And right there, coming through the door
Is a dress that once decked Clara Ward
A girdle follows, doing its best
To keep its place beneath that dress.
They've come back home in grand style
In a '57 Chevy --- a smile a mile!

The fun is loud, the music hot!
The dancin' makes them sweat a lot
A brownie camera catches it all
To hold these moments on the wall.

They partied hard all through the night
But now they're rushing to set things right
'Cause the doors will open very soon
And people will start to fill the rooms.

The family will be on its best behavior
Allowing everyone to savor
The feeling of a strong history
That the people seem so proud to see.

But with a secret wink each will remember
The night they jammed down to the bone
To celebrate their coming home
To the National Afro-American Museum
                        and Cultural Center.

TURKEY LEGS

for John Oliver Killens

Here's to turkey legs
we raised in a toast to Pushkin
sliced into chapters of
Wesley's first novel
with the sauce of Mervyn's
West Indian remembrances
Here's to turkey legs
braised like Youngblood

Thursdays at the Algonquin
we treated ourselves to
images smothered in the juices
of our imaginations

you brought lives into my life
dieties dancing across the plate
Richard Wright, Zora, Claude McKay
in the sparkle of your eyes
Mari Evans, Julian, Eloise G.
saints and sinners informed
Sterling, Owen, John Clarke
in your mischievious boy grin

new children
Askia, Carolyn
in a howl at the Cotillion
anxious children
Fatisha, George
belicose readers
with uneven sureness
hesitant voices
hovering in hangars
fueling ourselves on your
encouragement
You brought lives into my life

so here's to turkey legs, John
sending some over,
my treat.

THIRD ENTITY

the Ifa priest explains
that two ori (spirits/indwellers)
coming together merge into
a third entity.
Or, 1+1=3.

my ori
your ori
creating heart space
growin' we roots
bloomin' no blues
we wheat
     even the chaff is sweet
seedlings staring eye to eye
liking what we see
hugging trees
     that hum the songs
     of our mothers
     when they were lovers

This is no accident!
release the frightened breath
say Yes!
plant some love here
then come harvest me
so we be a 3rd entity

CALVIN R. HICKS

(hug)

i found it

of all places

under the bed. . . .

that hug

you left

i thought by mistake

until it

curled itself

around my toes

then i knew

you

left it there

on purpose.

FRESH

Hey, Fresh

I call you
Fresh
like a stolen nipple kiss
like a good cry
like a wailing note

Fresh.
like purple blueberries
an old Ashford & Simpson
song
a newborn's foot.

Fresh like tomorrow
    like a sunny rain
    a low down tingle
    a moving hand

    like a neck hug
    like a stroked thigh
Fresh like fast
    like fast
    like swifting
        on my body/heart

Hey, Fresh!

CALVIN R. HICKS

sweet

     time

sun

     time

wine

     time

song

     time

not enough

     time

then you are

gone

     time

GOOD-BYES and HELLOS   *four*

Don't go naked

into our tomorrow

Wrap yourself in love

Let it be right

Let it be grand

Let it be infinite.

GOOD NIGHTS

the earth moves
the sirens flare
a choir of car burglar alarms sings
om in six electronic keys
neighbors edge into the street
for the first time since . . .
the last time.
I sit on the broken step
release myself to the unquiet darkness
and bathe in the good nights.

> *"Oh Mary Mack, Mack, Mack*
> *All dressed in black, black, black*
> *With silver buttons, buttons, buttons*
> *All down her back, back, back . . . ."*

Cleveland nights
catching fireflies in Mason jars as
tenor crickets herald heat
another piece of Nana's lemon meringue pie
growing in a womb of all is well

> *"She asked her mother, mother, mother*
> *For fifteen cents, cents, cents*
> *To see the elephant, elephant, elephant*
> *Jump the fence, fence, fence . . . ."*

mesmerized by the talk of grown folks
please pretty please can I sleep
        on the porch tonight?
Good nights.

Camp nights
low coals and bronzed marshmallows
girl scout very american nights
bright girl voices
singing bonds, singing promises

> *"Follow, follow, follow the dream*
> *Of young and old, of green and gold*
> *Follow, follow, follow the dream . . ."*

firelight nights for dreamers
Good nights.

Addis Ababa nights
a taxi slips through the unstillness
racing against curfew
the melody of Ethiopia at the Hilton
still caressing my toes
I thank my driver for the Cinderella ride
say "Hello" in perfect Amharic
(I thought I said "good night" . . . .)
Good nights.

> *"The neon lights are always bright on Broadway*
> *Gonna be on Broadway, gonna be on Broadway,*
> *Gonna be on Broadway, gonna be on Broadway. . . . "*

Broadway nights
   the other Broadway
sidestepping police
their hips holding hands locked in prayer
around their penis clubs
congas riff off the roofs
proclaiming heat, sweat, territory
hot nights,
Good nights.

Harlem nights
the politically correct collect
at Kimako's
"Trying to make it real. . . .
            compared to what? . . . ."
Preachrighton! is a revolutionary sweet
the poets on a sugar high
heady with comprehension
and hope
and information ---
some secret is being born here
and we are all the designated godmother
with a Temptations sidestep
we move The Movement to
chicken & waffles at Wells'
the poets grease, and
(as we head back downtown)
mock the impatient dawn
with a Smokey song
Good nights.

Ouagadougou nights
kicking red dust in the sweaty softness
attentive to the heave of sleeping camels
feeling the muted music of the balafon
hold me to sleep
Good nights.

Antiqua nights
surrender my audience to slot machines
wild horses play nearby
watchful that I don't steal their berries
the laughter of the musicians bounces
off my back
as I lift my evening gown
to tease the Antiguan tide
singing nights
Good nights.

Surinam nights
toe dancing with the River that
splits the land
pulls it back together,
the River that holds the moon
the stars are warriors
telling me how they got ovah
We make a pact,
the Surinamese warriors and me
Good nights.

Ancestor nights
in the middle of Virginia's National Forest
the lovers dance with the ancestors
in celebration of having found each other
pretending it is Africa
pretending we are home
believing for a moment
that the actor in the white house
does not control this space
full moon love nights
Good nights.

Santa Ana nights
I whip barefoot like a kite
through the Pacific sand
singing my answers to the dark
A white dove swoops down from the South
drops the questions on
12 grains of sand
I thank Obatala.
This is a good night.

the earth moves
the firecrackers that mark
Satchmo's birthday
flare across
the stench of garbage
I sit on the broken step
release myself to the
whispering spirits
and bathe in the good nights.

                              earthquake Los Angeles
                              July 4th weekend

GERALD CYRUS

OUT OF THE DARKNESS

Out of the darkness
Out of the darkness i come
tip-toe
into the light
of the Third Eye.

Out of the darkness
Out of the darkness into the
Bright understanding
of my time.

At the edge of light
reach back
for the wisdom
deep black wisdom
for the word
coal black word.

Stepping in the tracks
my ancestors left
reading the trail they wove
on the leaves
on the seas
on my eyes' memory.

i'm coming
Out of the darkness
Out of the darkness
into the light
of the Third Eye.
Of the
Third Eye. . . . .
. . . . Ohmmmmmmm.

PHOTO CREDITS

NATHANIEL BELLAMY experiments in collage and hand-tinted photographic images at his loft in Los Angeles.
> Page 14   "Reflections of Inner Time"
> © Nathaniel Bellamy

GERALD CYRUS is a documentary photographer based in Los Angeles.
> Page 9   untitled
> Page 76   "Purification"
> © Gerald Cyrus

CALVIN R. HICKS is co-founder of the Black Photographer's Gallery in Los Angeles and personal photographer of "Queen Ethel."
> front cover "Nude Form"
> Page 32   "Queen Ethel," Mrs. Ethel Meeds at age 99
> Page 39   untitled
> Page 59   "Breakin'"
> Page 68,69   "Nude forms"
> back cover
> © Calvin R. Hicks 1990

ADELE HODGE is a TV news producer-turned-photographer in Chicago. Her photographs have appeared in *The Chicago Tribune* and *Essence.*
> Page 50   "Alisha"
> © Adele Hodge 1978

MEEDS FAMILY COLLECTION
> Page 53   Mrs. Ethel Meeds, at 101, after voting in the 1988 Presidential election.

SAUNDRA SHARP
> Page 26   aerialist Joanna Haigood in performance, 1988.
> Page 29   "Camp Colquitt, Central Avenue"
> Page 36   "Message on Washington Ave."
> Page 48   "Don't You Want To Look Like Me?"
> © Saundra Sharp

Photo consultant, Calvin R. Hicks
Cover design by Romeo Enriquez

ABOUT THE AUTHOR

Saundra Sharp has been writing poetry since she came out of a poet's womb in Cleveland, Ohio. Her collections include *From The Windows Of My Mind* (1970), *In The Midst Of Change* (1972) and *Soft Song*, (1978, reprinted by Harlem River Press, 1990.) She created the stage play *The Sistuhs* in the John O. Killens Writers Workshop in New York. For radio she's written more than 100 "infommercials" on African-American history, is publisher/editor of *The Black History Film List* (1987), and contributes to Black Film Review magazine. Her independent filmmaker credits include the shorts *Picking Tribes* and *Back Inside Herself*, and the documentary *Life Is A Saxophone*. Ms. Sharp starred in the television movies *Hollow Image* and *Minstrel Man*. She resides in Los Angeles where she is a volunteer literacy tutor.